Healthy HABITS™

Powerful Bones
Keeping Your Skeleton Healthy

Maria DaSilva-Gordon

rosen publishing's
rosen central®

New York

Dedicated to Alex, Sophia, and Maya. May you grow up to have strong and powerful bones.

Published in 2013 by The Rosen Publishing Group, Inc.
29 East 21st Street, New York, NY 10010

Library of Congress Cataloging-in-Publication Data

DaSilva-Gordon, Maria.
Powerful bones: keeping your skeleton healthy/Maria DaSilva-Gordon.—1st ed.
      p. cm.—(Healthy habits)
Includes bibliographical references and index.
ISBN 978-1-4488-6949-7 (library binding)
1. Bones—Juvenile literature. I. Title.
QP88.2.D37 2013
612.7'5—dc23

2011045469

Manufactured in the United States of America

CPSIA Compliance Information: Batch #S12YA: For further information, contact Rosen Publishing, New York, New York, at 1-800-237-9932.

CONTENTS

Introduction

Your bones do a lot for your body. They support you, protect you, allow you to move, and help your body perform all the activities required for daily living.

The bones in the body join together to form the skeleton. The skeleton acts like a frame for the body, giving it shape and support. Without bones, you wouldn't be able to walk, run, skip, or stand. You would be a blob of skin and soft tissue. Bones also protect the body. For example, the bones of the skull, or the cranial bones, protect the brain. The kneecap, or patella, protects the knee joint. And the ribs protect the heart and lungs.

Along with supporting and protecting the body, bones store minerals, including calcium and phosphorus. Acquired from the foods you eat, minerals make bones hard and strong. When other parts of the body need minerals for other uses, the bones release them into the blood.

Bones also allow you to move. Together with the muscles and joints in the body, bones make it possible for you to walk, play, dance, chew food, and perform various other movements.

Given everything your bones do, it's essential to keep them healthy and strong.

Your bones, along with your muscles and joints, help your body move and perform tasks such as jogging. In return, being active helps keep your bones strong.

What happens if you don't take care of your bones now? Later in life, your bones could become brittle and fracture easily, a condition called osteoporosis. You can reduce your risk of developing osteoporosis by getting enough calcium and vitamin D and engaging in regular, weight-bearing exercise. You can also keep your bones healthy by avoiding habits that damage bone, such as smoking, drinking heavily, dieting excessively, or becoming obese. Protecting bones from injury by using safety gear when taking part in sports or recreational activities and wearing a seatbelt in moving vehicles is also vital to your bone health.

By making healthy habits a part of your lifestyle, you can avoid or reduce the risk of bone problems. Eating right, getting enough exercise, and avoiding risky habits will help you have strong, powerful bones now and throughout your life.

Chapter 1

Powerful Bones: An Overview

Even though you might not think it when you feel how hard they are, bones are alive. Bones are made up of living cells, and they have a blood supply and a nerve supply. Just like other parts of the body, bones undergo growth and change. As you grow, everything about you gets bigger, including your bones. Your bones become longer, thicker, heavier, and denser.

Along with growing larger, bones also change in number. When you are born, you have about 300 bones. As you grow up, some of these bones grow together, or fuse. By the time you reach adulthood, you have 206 bones.

Bones also change throughout your life through a normal process called remodeling. In this process, special cells called osteoblasts break down bone tissue to release stored minerals that the body needs. Then cells called osteoclasts build new bone tissue to replace it.

Bone Anatomy

Bone is made up of different layers. The outer surface of bone is known as the periosteum. The first major layer of bone—the part you see when you look at a skeleton—is tough and dense. This layer is known as compact bone, or hard bone. If you could peek into the next layer, you would see what looks like a honeycomb or a sponge with many spaces. This area is called cancellous bone, or spongy bone. While cancellous bone isn't as hard as compact bone, it is still tough.

Bone marrow, which is a soft tissue, fills the center of many bones. Red bone marrow produces red blood cells, white blood cells, and blood platelets. Red blood cells transport oxygen to all parts of the body. White blood cells fight the germs that can make you sick. If you are injured, the platelets come together to help the blood to clot. In other words, if you cut yourself, your platelets "plug" the cut and stop the bleeding. Yellow bone marrow can send energy reserves, stored as fat, to other parts of the body if needed as a last resort.

Collagen is also found in most bones. A protein, collagen gives bone tissue a framework that is both flexible and strong. Bones are also made up of calcium and phosphorus, minerals that work together to make bones hard. Bones must be hard, but they must also be flexible to withstand stress without snapping.

Bones and Movement

In order to work properly, bones need some help. Joints are the places where two or more bones come together. The elbow is an example of a joint. Bones are held together at joints by ligaments, which are tough, elastic bands of tissue. Joints differ in size—some are big (such as the hip joint) and some are tiny (the smallest is found between two bones in the ear).

Joints also differ in how they move. Hinge joints, such as the knee, allow bones to move back and forth. Ball-and-socket joints, such as the shoulder joint, let bones move in all directions. Some joints in the

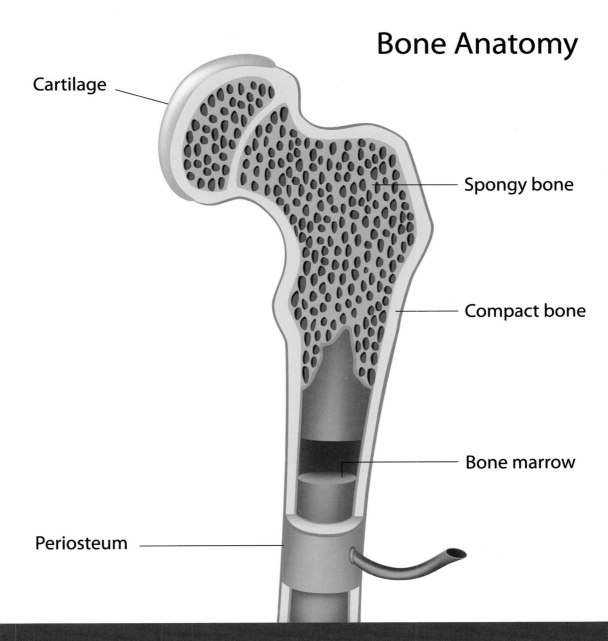

Bone Anatomy

Cartilage

Spongy bone

Compact bone

Bone marrow

Periosteum

From the periosteum—the membrane on the outer surface of the bone—to the bone marrow that fills the center, bone is made up of different layers.

body, like those found in the skull, don't move at all. These are known as fixed joints.

The bones are also able to move thanks to the muscles that are attached to them. The muscles are attached to bones by tendons, cords of tough tissue. When the muscles contract, they pull on the tendons and move the bones.

Cartilage also plays a role in movement. Tough but bendable, cartilage can be found in various parts of the body, including the joints. Found at the ends of bones, this connective tissue prevents bones from rubbing together, absorbs shock, and provides moisture. You can find examples of cartilage by simply touching the tops of your ears or the tip of your nose.

Building Up Your Bone Bank

Bones are living organs that constantly change. Old bone tissue is broken down to release minerals that the body needs, and new bone tissue is created to replace it. The amount of bone tissue in the skeleton is known as bone mass.

During the childhood and teenage years, there is more bone tissue being created than being broken down. The amount of bone mass a person has when the skeleton reaches full maturation is known as peak bone mass. The process reverses as a person gets older. Starting in a person's late thirties, more bone is being broken down than created.

Think of your bone tissue like an allowance: the more you save now, the more you will have for later. Instead of saving in order to buy the latest must-have item, however, you are saving in order to have strong, healthy bones throughout your life. As your skeleton increases in density and size during your childhood and teenage years, there is more bone being "saved," or created, than "spent," or broken down. According to the National Institutes of Health (NIH), by the time girls turn eighteen and boys turn twenty, they have typically reached up to 90 percent of their peak bone mass. By about age thirty, most people have reached 100 percent of their peak bone mass. This means that their bones have become as strong and dense as they will ever be.

Now is the best time to start "saving" bone tissue. The amount of bone mass you gain during childhood and adolescence will influence the health of your skeleton for the rest of your life.

After your mid-30s, you begin to slowly lose bone mass. Women lose bone mass faster after menopause, but it happens to men, too.

Bone Growth/Loss

Active Growth

Slow Loss

Rapid Loss

Less Rapid Loss

10 20 30 40 50 60 70 80 90
Age in Years

During the childhood and teenage years, more bone tissue is being created than broken down, making this the best time to build strong, healthy bones for life.

Nutrition and Exercise

Some of the factors that affect peak bone mass, like those listed in the sidebar on page 14, are things that you can't change. However, you do have control over other factors, such as what you eat and how much exercise you get each day.

Eating right is one of the most important ways to keep your bones healthy. Eat foods that are high in calcium, a vital nutrient for bone health. Young people who don't get enough calcium may increase their risk for bone fractures when they are older. They may also lower their peak bone mass by 5 to 10 percent, according to the NIH.

Being physically active is also vital for building healthy bones. The more bones are used, the stronger they become. The importance of nutrition and exercise will be discussed in greater detail in the coming chapters.

Osteoporosis

By eating right and exercising regularly, you can have a positive effect on your peak bone mass. Why is it so important to "save" your bone-tissue allowance now? Later in life, low levels of bone tissue could lead to problems such as osteoporosis. A condition that causes bones to become weak and more likely to break, osteoporosis most commonly occurs in people over age sixty-five, but it can also affect younger people. In osteoporosis, bones lose minerals and become thin and fragile.

Because bone-tissue loss happens over a long period of time and usually without any initial symptoms, people are often unaware that they have osteoporosis until it is advanced. The first sign that someone has osteoporosis can be when a bone breaks. At that point, the disease can be extremely painful.

Most fractures related to osteoporosis occur in bones that support a person's weight—the hips or vertebrae (the bones of the spine). Sometimes, older people with osteoporosis experience a hip or vertebral fracture without even falling or having an accident. In these instances, the bones become so weak that they start collapsing under

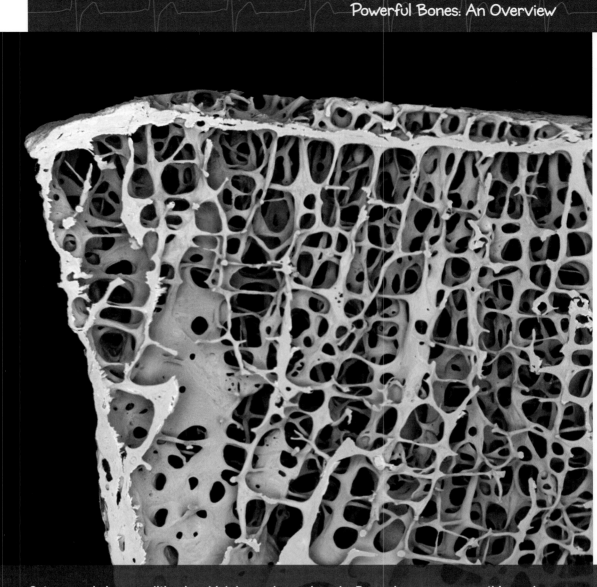

Osteoporosis is a condition in which bones lose minerals. Bones become porous, thin, and brittle to the point of breaking. Eating right and exercising can help prevent this disease.

the person's weight. Bones can become so brittle that simply coughing or bending over can cause a bone to break. Following a severe bone injury, some older people lose their ability to sit up, stand, or walk. Bone injuries from osteoporosis can lead to hospitalization, placement in a nursing home, and even death.

You may have noticed that some older people seem to get shorter over time. People with weak bones in their spines gradually lose height. They become hunched over as the weakened spine begins to bend.

Osteoporosis is both common and costly. According to the U.S. Department of Health and Human Services, each year 1.5 million older Americans suffer fractures from weak bones. The cost of treating these broken bones is as high as $18 billion per year.

Factors that Affect Peak Bone Mass

According to the NIH, there are a number of factors that affect peak bone mass. Along with nutrition, exercise, and other habits, the following factors can play a role:

- **Gender.** On average, males have a greater bone mass than females. This isn't true in childhood. Before reaching puberty, boys and girls acquire bone mass at almost the same rates. However, after puberty, males typically reach a higher peak bone mass than females.
- **Race.** Compared to Caucasian and Asian girls, African American girls typically acquire greater peak bone mass. The reasons why are still unclear. African American females also have a lower risk for osteoporosis as they age.
- **Hormones.** Sex hormones such as estrogen play a vital role in bone mass development. Greater bone density is typically found among girls who start menstruating at an early age. Girls who regularly miss their menstrual periods may lose bone density.

Reducing Your Risk

The size and density of your bones help determine their strength. Bone density is determined, in part, by how much calcium is in your bones. Therefore, one of the best things you can do to help prevent osteoporosis is to consume enough calcium. On the flip side, if you go through life without getting enough calcium, you increase your risk for getting osteoporosis. Being physically active also helps reduce a person's likelihood of developing this disease. Bones respond to weight-bearing physical activity by growing stronger.

While osteoporosis occurs in both men and women, females tend to get the disease more often. On average, women have thinner and weaker bones than men. Women are also more vulnerable to the disease because of hormonal changes that occur later in life.

Family history and heredity also play a role in determining a person's risk for developing osteoporosis. If you have a parent or sibling with osteoporosis, especially if you also have a family history of fractures, your risk is greater.

Unfortunately, there is no cure for this disease, only prevention, which is why "saving" as much bone tissue as possible now is so important—particularly for girls. Bones grow the fastest during the tween and teen years. The more bone tissue you "save" during this time, the less likely you are to develop weak and broken bones now and later in life.

Chapter 2

Eating for Bone Health

Proper nutrition plays a crucial part in bone health. It's important to get enough calcium in your diet each day. A mineral, calcium helps build strong bones. Calcium also helps muscles to contract, blood to clot, and nerves to send messages.

Nearly all of the calcium in the body is stored in the bones and teeth. Calcium is deposited and withdrawn from the bones every day. If you do not get enough calcium from food, when the body needs calcium, it is taken from your "bone bank" and released into the bloodstream. If your diet is too low in calcium, you may end up withdrawing more calcium than you deposit.

Getting Enough Calcium

How much calcium should you be taking in each day? The amount depends on your age. According to the Institute of Medicine (IOM), children ages one to three need 700 milligrams (mg) of calcium per day. Children between the ages of four and eight need 1,000 mg per day. From ages nine to eighteen, adolescents need a total of 1,300 mg of calcium every day.

Unfortunately, most children and teens aren't getting enough calcium. According to the National Institute of Child Health and Human Development, only one in four boys ages nine to thirteen consumes enough calcium daily. For girls in this age group, the numbers are worse: less than one in ten girls gets enough calcium each day. You can't make up for low calcium intake in youth when you get older, so it is important to get the recommended amount now.

The best way to reach the daily calcium requirement is to consume calcium-rich foods. Common sources of calcium are milk and other dairy products, such as cheese, single-serve puddings, and yogurt.

Drinking milk is one of the easiest ways to reach your calcium requirement for the day. Not only is milk a calcium-rich food, the calcium is in a form that the body can easily absorb. By drinking just one serving of milk each day—8 fluid ounces, or 1 cup (250 milliliters)—a person

Calcium plays a key role in building strong bones. One way to make sure you are getting enough of this essential mineral every day is to drink milk.

can get approximately 300 mg of calcium. That's nearly one quarter of the total amount of calcium tweens and teens need for the day.

Best of all, low-fat and nonfat milk options provide the calcium a person needs, minus the added fat from whole milk. While children ages one to two should drink whole milk, anyone older should drink low-fat or nonfat milk. With obesity in children and adults a nationwide concern, it's important to avoid adding extra fat to your diet whenever possible.

If you don't like drinking milk on its own, try having milk with your favorite cereal. (Choose a cereal with added calcium for an even bigger calcium boost.) When making oatmeal, opt for milk instead of water. Or, you can try adding milk to a fruit smoothie.

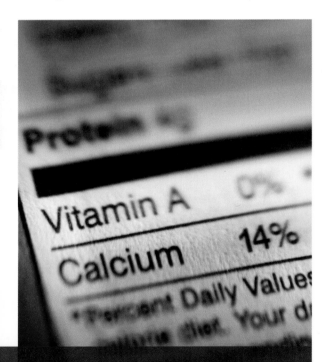

Food labels tell you the percent daily value of calcium in one serving of the product. One serving of this food provides 14 percent of the calcium an adult needs for the day.

Reading Food Labels

To find out how much calcium different foods contain, check food labels. Food labels are found on packaged products under the heading "Nutrition Facts." This label tells you the calcium content of a food based on a single serving size—and one serving isn't necessarily the same as the entire package. Food labels also provide information such as the amount of calories, fat, and protein in each serving.

By reading food labels, you can easily find out which foods are calcium-rich and which foods are not. Foods rich in calcium have a 20 percent daily value or higher.

On food labels, the amount of calcium isn't listed in milligrams (mg) but as a percentage of the daily value (%DV). The daily value is the total amount of a nutrient that a typical adult on a two thousand calorie diet needs per day. The percent daily value tells how much one serving of the food contributes toward the total needed.

So which foods qualify as good sources of calcium? The U.S. Food and Drug Administration (FDA) shares a guideline called the "5-20 rule" for important nutrients. Foods with about a 5 percent daily value for calcium are considered low in calcium. Foods with a 20 percent daily value or higher are considered calcium-rich.

Calcium-Rich Foods

There are a number of different foods you can eat to meet the calcium requirement for adolescents—1,300 mg daily. Below is a list of calcium-rich foods, their serving sizes, and the amount of calcium in each serving. Keep in mind that the amount of calcium listed for each food is an estimate and not an exact number. Different brands sometimes use different ingredients, which can cause a food to have slightly more or less calcium.

FOOD	SERVING SIZE	CALCIUM (mg)
Plain yogurt, nonfat	1 cup (245 g)	452
Soy drink with calcium added	1 cup (236.5 mL)	368
Fruit yogurt, low-fat	1 cup (245 g)	343
American cheese, pasteurized	2 ounces (56.6 g)	323
Mozzarella, part skim	1 ½ ounces (42.5 g)	311
Orange juice with calcium	1 cup (236.5 mL)	300
Spinach, cooked	½ cup (90 g)	122
Frozen yogurt, soft-serve, vanilla	½ cup (72 g)	103
Dry cereal with calcium	1 cup (28 g)	100–1,000 (amounts vary)
White beans, canned	½ cup (131 g)	96
Almonds, dry roasted	1 ounce (28.35 g)	76
Broccoli, cooked	1 cup (156 g)	62

Keep in mind that the percent daily value is based on the amount of calcium adults ages nineteen to fifty need each day—1,000 mg total. Adolescents ages nine to eighteen require more calcium than that—1,300 mg daily. Teens who want to determine if they are getting enough calcium can use the following formula: the percent daily value of calcium of all foods should equal 130 percent or more.

Another way to track your calcium intake is to convert each food's percent daily value for calcium into milligrams. Luckily, the calculation is simple. To convert the percent daily value into milligrams, just multiply by ten, or add a zero. For instance, if the label lists the calcium content for a serving of food as 20 percent daily value (20%DV), this means it contains 200 mg of calcium (20 x 10 = 200). (This calculation works only for calcium and not for other nutrients listed on food labels.)

To ensure you are getting enough calcium every day (1,300 mg), aim for four servings of foods that each have 300 mg of calcium (30% DV). Or, you can set a goal of six to seven servings of foods with 200 mg of calcium (20%DV). To make up for any shortfalls in calcium intake, also include some foods that have a lower percent daily value for calcium.

Vitamin D

In addition to calcium, other nutrients like vitamin D help keep bones strong and healthy. Vitamin D helps the body absorb calcium from the foods you eat. Vitamin D can be found in egg yolks and fatty fish such as salmon and tuna. Milk and milk products fortified with vitamin D are another good source of this vitamin. To find out if vitamin D has been added to other products such as breads and cereals, read the food labels. According to the IOM, for people ages one to seventy, the recommended daily amount of vitamin D is 600 international units (IU), or 15 micrograms.

Did you know you can get vitamin D from sunlight? The body produces vitamin D when the skin is exposed to the sun. Playing an outdoor sport is an ideal way to get vitamin D and the exercise you

Taking part in an outdoor sport such as tennis strengthens bones, and the sun exposure helps the body produce vitamin D.

need to keep your bones strong. Just fifteen to twenty minutes in the sun two to three times a week is considered enough time. If you plan to be outside longer, be sure to wear sunscreen. Too much exposure to the sun's ultraviolet rays is not healthy for your skin.

Taking supplements can be another way to get enough vitamin D. However, be sure to check with your doctor before taking any kind of supplement.

Getting the right amount of vitamin D is important. Not getting enough could lead to a deficiency. In children, vitamin D deficiency causes a disease known as rickets, which causes the bones to become soft and bend. While rarer today than in the past, the disease still does occur.

Getting too much vitamin D can also cause problems. When amounts in the blood become too high, people can develop vitamin D toxicity, or poisoning. Symptoms of toxicity include nausea, weakness, weight loss, and vomiting. In most cases, the overuse of supplements is the cause of vitamin D toxicity. When in doubt about how much of a vitamin or mineral to take, check with your doctor.

When Milk Isn't an Option

For people with a milk allergy, consuming milk isn't an option. One of the most common food allergies among children, a milk allergy means you are allergic to one or both types of protein found in cow's milk— whey and casein. People who are allergic to milk need to avoid all milk products and milk proteins. Dairy products such as yogurt, cheese, and butter are off-limits.

People who are allergic to milk and consume it can experience various symptoms, such as wheezing, cramps, vomiting, or a skin rash. In some rare cases, a milk allergy can result in anaphylaxis, a reaction that can cause airways to narrow and breathing to become

Calcium-fortified orange juice is a great alternative for those who must avoid milk and other dairy products.

blocked. For many of those with a milk allergy, consuming even a small amount of milk is out of the question.

Fortunately, there are plenty of alternatives. People who have to avoid dairy products can choose other calcium-rich foods, such as almonds, spinach, and bok choy. There are many milk-free foods available that are calcium-fortified, or have calcium added to them. Some examples of calcium-fortified options include certain orange juices, breads, cereals, and soy beverages. Just remember: before trying any new food product, people with food allergies should read the label carefully to check for any problem ingredients. Taking calcium supplements is another option for someone who has difficulty getting enough calcium; however, the preferred source is from foods.

Lactose Intolerance

While a milk allergy involves the immune system, lactose intolerance involves the digestive system. People with this condition can't fully digest lactose, the milk sugar in dairy products. For people with lactose intolerance, consuming foods that contain lactose can cause nausea, cramps, diarrhea, gas, or bloating.

There is no cure for lactose intolerance. However, there are ways for people to reduce their symptoms and still get enough calcium. For example, they can try eating dairy products in small amounts (less than the normal serving size). Instead of drinking milk on its own, they can consume it with other foods to slow the digestive process.

Since all dairy products are not the same, individuals might tolerate some foods better than others. For instance, hard, aged cheeses such as cheddar have less lactose and may cause fewer symptoms. Yogurt may be an option because the bacterial cultures in it help break down lactose. People can further limit symptoms by choosing food products that are lactose-free or lactose-reduced. Taking lactase enzyme tablets or drops can also help the body digest dairy products.

Some people with lactose intolerance may have to avoid all dairy products. Like people with milk protein allergies, they can get calcium from nondairy foods and supplements.

Consequences of Poor Nutrition

Making poor nutrition choices can have negative consequences for your bones. Take, for example, foods that are high in salt. Consuming high-sodium foods causes the body to lose calcium and can result in bone loss. To prevent this from happening, cut back on eating foods that have been canned or processed. Also, avoid adding salt to the foods you eat. You can determine if a food has a high amount of salt by reading the food label. Foods that have a salt content of 20 percent daily value or higher are considered high-sodium foods.

According to the National Osteoporosis Foundation, some studies suggest that drinking colas and other caffeinated drinks such

Guzzling colas and other caffeinated drinks may lead to weaker bones. Instead, opt for milk and calcium-fortified drinks as your beverages of choice.

as coffee may lead to weaker bones. The connection between these beverages and bone loss might simply be due to people choosing them over milk and calcium-fortified drinks, and thus consuming less calcium. On the other hand, it is possible that compounds in colas and coffee contribute to bone loss. More research is needed to know for sure. When it comes to beverages, play it safe and choose milk and calcium-fortified drinks over colas and coffee.

Eating disorders can also lead to bone health problems. Disorders like anorexia nervosa, in which people limit what they eat and become too thin, can lead to missed or irregular periods in females after puberty. It can also lead to a condition known as amenorrhea, in which females stop having periods altogether. Major disruptions in the menstrual cycle can lead to low estrogen—an important hormone for bone health. Estrogen plays a key role in the development of bone density and in reaching peak bone mass. Girls who are anorexic may experience fractures as a result of weak bones. They also greatly increase their risk of developing osteoporosis and fractures later in life. If their eating disorders are severe, girls can develop osteoporosis as early as in their twenties.

A recent study indicates that being obese may also be bad for your bones. A 2007 study at the University of Georgia found that participants with high body fat had bones that were 8 to 9 percent weaker than those of participants with normal body fat. This finding was surprising to the researchers. Muscles apply force on bones, which encourages bone growth. Because obese people tend to have more muscle surrounding their bones, researchers had expected obese participants would have stronger bones, not weaker ones. While the reasons for the findings are still unclear, studies with obese rats have shown that they produce more fat cells in the bone marrow and fewer bone cells.

While bones can be tough, they need your help to reach their full potential and to stay strong. Eating right and maintaining a healthy weight will help keep your bones healthy in the years to come.

10 Great Questions
to Ask a Health Professional

1. How do you measure a person's bone mass?

2. How can I increase my calcium intake?

3. How do I know if I'm getting enough vitamin D?

4. What is the most common type of fracture, and how can I prevent it?

5. What are the symptoms of an overuse injury?

6. What are growth plate injuries, and how can I prevent them?

7. Where can I get help for an eating disorder?

8. How can I overcome obesity?

9. How do I know if I'm ready to start a strength-training program?

10. Where can I get help for a problem with excessive exercising?

Chapter 3

How Exercise Can Help

In addition to eating right, getting enough exercise each day plays an important role in keeping bones healthy. Like muscles, bones get stronger with exercise. Physical activity on a regular basis stimulates the bones to produce more bone tissue.

Weight-Bearing Activities

When it comes to bone health, not all exercise is the same. To benefit bones, people need to take part in weight-bearing activities. These kinds of activities help determine the shape, strength, and mass of bone.

If your legs support your body weight when you are active, you are taking part in a weight-bearing activity. Weight-bearing activities include walking, running, jumping rope, and gymnastics. Other weight-bearing activities include dancing, hiking, climbing, and playing tag outside with friends. Sports like basketball, soccer, tennis, softball, and volleyball are also great weight-bearing activities. While exercises like swimming and cycling will help keep you fit, they don't require your legs to carry your body weight. Therefore, they aren't considered weight-bearing activities.

Volleyball is a great way to get exercise, have fun, and build stronger bones. Whenever the legs support a person's body weight during an activity, the bones benefit.

Strength Training for Bone Benefits

Another area of fitness that offers bone benefits is strength training. Strength training not only helps with bone development, it also increases muscle strength and endurance and helps protect the muscles and joints from injury.

Strength training is different from weight lifting or bodybuilding, in which participants often compete to build the biggest muscles and lift the most weight. Weight lifting and bodybuilding can put too much strain on young tendons, muscles, and growth plates (areas of cartilage that haven't turned to bone yet). Instead, strength training uses light resistance and controlled movements. The focus is on proper technique, form, and safety—not on how much weight you can lift.

Think you're too young to start doing strength training? You can start a supervised strength-training program as early as age eight if you are mature enough, can follow directions, and can maintain proper balance and posture. You also need the motivation to train several times a week. You can do strength-training exercises using your own body weight, resistance tubing, a medicine ball, or light weights. Activities such as yoga, Pilates, and gymnastics can also help to build strength.

Before you begin strength training, be sure to check with a health professional first. To get started, work with someone who has experience with youth strength training or take a strength-training class for your age group. The program you follow should be one that is age-appropriate. Your body isn't the same as an adult's, so you shouldn't take part in a program aimed at adults.

In strength training, exercises focus on strengthening the muscles in various body parts, such as the legs, hips, back, chest, stomach,

Through the use of light resistance and controlled movements, strength training not only benefits your bones, it also increases muscle strength and endurance.

arms, and shoulders. Examples of muscle-strengthening exercises include push-ups, sit-ups, squats, lunges, and working with resistance bands. Typically, each exercise is repeated eight to twelve times in a row. Each move is often called a "rep," or repetition. The group of eight to twelve reps is known as a "set."

If you don't think you will see any results from strength training until after you hit puberty, think again. According to the American Academy of Pediatrics, young athletes who take part in a well-designed strength-training program for at least eight weeks will see a 30 to 50 percent increase in strength. This increase in strength is noticeable in how the

Safe Strength Training

As with any activity, strength training can result in injury. You can reduce your risk of injury by taking part in a well-supervised strength-training program with a qualified adult. Listening and following instructions will also help prevent injury, as will the following tips:

- Be sure to wear appropriate clothing and closed-toe athletic shoes.
- Start your workout with a five- to ten-minute warm-up. Walking, running in place, or jumping rope are good options.
- If you are training with machines, make sure they have been adjusted for your height.
- Work slowly, focusing on correct form and technique.
- Don't hold your breath or breathe too quickly while performing the exercises.
- Be sure to take rests between sets to allow your body to get its energy back.
- If you feel pain when doing an exercise, stop immediately and tell an adult.
- End the session the way it began, with five to ten minutes of light activity.
- To avoid dehydration, drink water before you begin, during the workout, and afterward.

Also, before and after a strength-training session—or any type of exercise—be sure to stretch. Stretching can help improve flexibility, which, in turn, may decrease your risk of injury. To avoid injury while stretching, never stretch cold muscles. Instead, stretch after warming up and after you exercise.

muscles work, not in increased muscle size. You may not see results right away, but when you do, you'll be pleased with the positive changes in your muscle strength and endurance. Your bones will thank you, too.

Get the Right Amount of Exercise

You now know that weight-bearing activities and strength training are good for your bones. You also know that being physically active is important for your bone health. But how much exercise is enough? On most days of the week, if not all, children and adolescents should get at least sixty minutes of physical activity. This can be a combination of weight-bearing and muscle strengthening activities, including those you might not think of as working out, such as doing yard chores or playing on a jungle gym. Your total amount of physical activity can be accumulated by taking part in several fifteen-minute bouts of activity throughout the day. Without physical activity—and especially during long periods of inactivity—you could experience a loss of bone mass.

On the other hand, getting too much exercise isn't a good thing for your bones either, particularly

When you eat too little, the body doesn't get the nutrition it needs to function normally. Without enough calcium, bone loss can occur.

for females. Occasionally, female athletes intent on being thin or light-weight may exercise too much and/or eat too little. As a result, they might develop one or more of the following conditions: disordered eating, menstrual dysfunction, and premature (early) osteoporosis. These conditions are related to one another.

Disordered eating can take many forms, such as self-starvation (anorexia nervosa), overeating and purging (bulimia), and abuse of drugs such as diet pills, laxatives, or diuretics. Disordered eating prevents the body from getting the proper nutrition. This can cause various problems, such as fatigue, muscle weakness, dehydration, kidney damage, and erratic heartbeat. A lack of calcium can lead to bone loss during a time in life when a person should be building bone, not losing it.

Menstrual dysfunction, or problems with a female's periods, can also harm bone health. Excessive exercising or poor nutrition can cause periods to be missed, to become irregular, or to stop—signs of low estrogen. Physical or emotional stress, a low percentage of body fat, and a low calorie intake are other factors that can cause menstrual dysfunction. When there is a lack of regular menstruation, or periods, the body's bone-building processes are disrupted, and the skeleton weakens. Low levels of the hormone estrogen can result in bone density loss and a loss in strength. As a result, bones are more likely to break. This is known as premature osteoporosis.

In the worst-case scenario, exercising too much and/or eating too little can cause long-term damage to bones. It can also lead to death.

Exercising or dieting excessively can also have a negative effect on a person's athletic performance. The athlete might even have to limit or stop exercising. If you think you have been exercising excessively, have developed abnormal eating patterns, have experienced a stress fracture while playing a sport, or have missed several periods, it's important to reach out to a trusted adult for help.

Getting the right kind of exercise and the right amount of exercise is important for healthy, strong bones. You should aim for sixty minutes of exercise each day, making sure to spend some of that time doing weight-bearing activities. By incorporating weight-bearing activities and strength training into your lifestyle, you'll be on your way to building strong bones. Plus, you'll enjoy the additional benefits exercise offers, such as stress reduction and maintenance of a healthy weight.

MYTHS and FACTS

Strength training will stunt my growth.
According to the American Academy of Pediatrics (AAP), there are no indications that children who take part in resistance exercises on a regular basis will have growth plate damage or stop growing. In fact, strength training—when done regularly with correct form and technique, qualified supervision, low weights, and high repetitions—has a positive outcome on bone growth and development. Research has even shown that strength training is safer than playing basketball, football, and soccer.

Strength training is for athletes only.
Strength training offers benefits to athletes and nonathletes alike. For athletes,

strength training may improve sports performance and can reduce the risk of sports-related injuries. For nonathletes, strength training helps participants look and feel better and build greater strength and endurance. For young people who are overweight, strength training helps increase metabolism and lean body mass. For all participants, strength training offers the benefit of strong, healthy bones and muscles.

MYTH

Drinking and eating dairy products will make me fat.

FACT

There are plenty of low-fat and nonfat dairy products available. These products not only provide you with the calcium you need to keep your bones healthy, but they do it without adding fat to your diet. Try drinking skim milk or low-fat milk and eating low-fat cheese and yogurt. You can also get your calcium from nondairy (and low-fat) choices such as green leafy vegetables and calcium-fortified juices.

Chapter 4

Protecting Your Bones from Injury

As an adolescent, your bones, ligaments, muscles, and tendons are still growing, and certain parts of the bones are susceptible to injury. Because of this, it's especially important to be careful when you are physically active. By following safety guidelines and the tips in this chapter, you can reduce your risk of bone and muscle injuries.

Playing It (Extra) Safe

One of the best ways to prevent injuries while participating in an activity is to wear appropriate protective gear. For example, if you are going for a bike ride, be sure to wear a helmet.

Warming up before playing a sport is another way to reduce the risk of injury. When you do five to ten minutes of light aerobic activity, such as walking, jogging in place, or jumping rope, you are preparing your body for the physical demands of the activity. A warm-up gets your blood flowing, increases your breathing rate, and raises your muscle temperature. Gentle stretching can also be incorporated into your warm-up.

When taking part in a sport, make sure you fully understand the rules of the game. It's important to follow these rules. If you don't, you risk injuring not only yourself but also others who are playing with you.

To help prevent injury, be sure to warm up before taking part in an activity. Gentle stretching, along with light aerobic activity, can be part of your warm-up.

If you are too tired to play, don't. Playing when you are too tired increases your chance of making a mistake, which could lead to an injury. You also shouldn't play if you are in pain. You could end up turning a minor injury into a major one.

Before playing a sport, make sure you can physically meet the demands of the activity. For example, if you can't run around for long periods of time without feeling out of breath, chances are you aren't ready to play soccer. You might need to practice more and improve physically before you can take part in a sport.

Top Injury-Producing Activities

While any activity poses a risk for injury, the following four cause the most injuries to bones and muscles in youth: bicycling, basketball, football, and roller sports. According to the American Academy of Orthopaedic Surgeons (AAOS), these activities cause an estimated 1.5 million medically treated injuries each year among children ages five to fourteen.

According to AAOS, the recreational activity that sees the highest number of injuries a year—415,000—is bicycle riding. Most injuries are bruises, but broken arms and wrists are also common. To prevent

Take precautions to avoid injury while participating in roller sports such as inline skating. Wear protective gear such as helmets, knee pads, and elbow pads.

injuries associated with this activity, take a riding skills course, don't ride at night, avoid uneven or slippery surfaces, and always wear a helmet.

The team sport that sees the highest number of injuries is basketball, with 407,000 bone and muscle injuries each year. While boys and girls in the five-to-fourteen age group have similar injury rates, girls fifteen and older have a higher rate of knee injuries. Ankle sprains are also more common in girls than in boys. To prevent basketball-related injuries, wear protective equipment such as a mouth guard or ankle braces. Focusing on good form will also help prevent injury. For example, to avoid knee-related injuries, land on a bent knee instead of a straight knee after jumping for a ball.

Football accounts for about 389,000 bone and muscle injuries each year, according to AAOS. Fractures are common injuries in this sport. To avoid injury, participants should wear protective equipment, drink lots of fluids, and practice proper technique—such as tackling an opponent without using the head and neck.

Roller sports, which include skateboarding, riding scooters, roller-skating, and inline skating, cause 297,000 medically treated bone and muscle injuries per year. More than 125,000 injuries involve broken bones, and many of them occur in children younger than ten. Skateboarding-related fractures are common in children ages eleven to fourteen. To prevent injuries related to roller sports, wear protective equipment, practice tricks in a safe environment with adult supervision, and opt for smooth surfaces away from traffic.

Types of Injuries

Despite your best efforts, you still might experience an injury. After all, accidents do happen. Among young athletes, there are two main types of injuries to bones, muscles, and ligaments: acute injuries and over-use injuries. Acute injuries are caused by sudden trauma such as a fall, twist, or collision. Common acute injuries among children include fractures, strains, sprains, and bruises.

Overuse injuries are caused by repeated stresses to a body part. The results can range from minor fractures and muscle tears to pro-gressive bone deformities. Whereas acute injuries are typically the result of a specific incident, overuse injuries tend to develop over a period of time. Children who do a lot of throwing, like pitchers in base-ball, may experience overuse injuries.

Regardless of the type of injury you have, it's important to seek medical care. In some cases, leaving an injury untreated could cause issues with your physical growth and lead to permanent damage.

Fractures

The medical term for a broken bone is a fracture. Bone fractures can result from an accident during a sport or recreational activity. They can also result from a traumatic event such as a fall or car collision. Symptoms of fractures include hearing a snap or a pop, sweating, nausea, immediate swelling, tingling, bruising, and pain when you move the injured area. Sometimes, however, you may not have the typical symptoms associated with fractures.

If you think you might have a fracture, you should get help imme-diately. You should also avoid moving the injured bone. Moving a broken bone is painful, and it might worsen the injury to the bone as well as to surrounding tissue, vessels, and nerves. (Broken bones are very sharp.) You will likely have to get an X-ray of the area to deter-mine if there is a broken bone and, if so, where it is and what kind of fracture it is.

Types of Bone Fractures

There are several different types of fractures. A doctor will determine which kind of fracture has occurred by examining the patient and getting an X-ray image of the bone to confirm the diagnosis.

- **Simple fracture.** In a simple, or closed, fracture, the bone is broken, but the skin is not pierced.
- **Compound fracture.** A compound, or open, fracture means the bone has broken through the skin. Infection can occur and spread rapidly though the bone. This can delay healing of the fracture.
- **Comminuted fracture.** In this type of fracture, the bone shatters into more than two pieces, or it is crushed.
- **Greenstick fracture.** The bone bends, but it does not break into two pieces. This type of fracture occurs most often in children, whose bones are softer and more pliable.
- **Oblique fracture.** Oblique fractures result from twisting injuries and have a curved or angled shape.
- **Stress fracture.** This is a hairline crack in a bone. Common among athletes, stress fractures can result from overuse.

Blood vessels and cells that work to repair broken bones are found in the periosteum, the membrane on the outer surface of bones. When a bone breaks, the space between the broken ends of the bone is sealed by a blood clot, a mass of blood that has hardened from a liquid to a solid. Then, a couple of days later, the periosteum goes to

X-rays help doctors confirm if you have a broken bone, where it is located, and what kind of fracture you have. This X-ray shows an arm with multiple fractures.

work. Bone-producing cells from the periosteum work to seal the break by creating new bone between the ends of the fracture. This new bone is called bone callus.

Although broken bones have the ability to repair themselves, they often need outside help in order to heal in the right position. Failure to heal correctly can result in decreased functioning and chronic (ongoing) pain.

If the ends of the injured bone no longer meet the way they should (known as a displaced or misaligned fracture), a doctor will have to place the bone back in the correct position. In some cases, the doctor can simply set the bone with his or her hands. In other cases, he or she may need to perform surgery. The doctor may insert metal pins to keep the bone from moving while it heals properly. (The pins are sometimes removed after the bone has healed.)

Once the broken bone has been set, a cast is typically placed over the injured area to keep the bone in place. The most common type of cast is made of bandages that have been soaked in plaster. The bandages harden around the body part. Other types of casts are made of fiberglass or plastic.

The amount of time it will take the bone to heal depends on factors such as the type of break, the location of the break, your age, and your bone health. After the break mends—usually in one to two months for young people—the cast is removed. The body part that was in a cast might look different. It might be very pale. It might look smaller because you've had to rest the area and, as a result, have lost some muscle. (Muscles atrophy, or shrink, when you don't use them.) Fortunately, the unsightly appearance of your body part is temporary, and it will eventually look normal again.

Once the cast is removed, it will likely take some time for you to ease back into your normal physical activities. Your doctor might have you

A physician's assistant watches an X-ray monitor while setting a child's leg fracture in a Colorado hospital. Physicians can sometimes set broken bones by using their hands. In other cases, surgery is needed.

perform strengthening exercises or go to physical therapy to restore flexibility and strength.

Growth Plate Injuries

It is also possible to injure your growth plates, the areas of cartilage in the body that are still developing into bone. Growth plates are found at the ends of long bones, such as the bones in the legs. Also known as epiphyseal plates, growth plates influence the future length and shape of the bone. During adolescence, the growth plates are eventually replaced by solid bone.

The growth plates are not strong. In fact, they are the weakest parts of the growing skeleton. As a result, growth plates can be fractured easily. Many growth plate injuries occur when children are taking part in recreational activities or competitive sports. Growth plate injuries can also be caused by a traumatic event such as a fall or car accident. Overuse can also lead to growth plate injuries. Boys experience growth plate fractures twice as often as girls do because their bodies don't mature as quickly. The growth plates in girls turn to bone sooner than the growth plates in boys do.

Growth plate injuries require immediate medical attention. If a growth plate fracture isn't treated properly, it can lead to improper bone growth and function. How a growth plate injury is treated and heals depends on the type of injury, the severity of the injury, your age, and how much bone growth you have left before reaching adulthood. Typically, treatment features a combination of the following: immobilizing the injured bone by putting it in a cast or a splint, setting the bone through surgery or manipulation by hand, performing muscle-strengthening and range-of-motion exercises, and long-term follow-up.

Fortunately, according to the NIH, about 85 percent of growth plate fractures heal without any long-term problems. Sometimes, however, the fracture can cause the injured bone to stop growing. In such cases, bone growth is stunted, and the injured bone ends up being shorter than the uninjured bone in the opposite limb. Whether or not this happens depends on the type of fracture, the treatment received, and other factors, such as how severe the injury is and which growth plate is affected.

After a broken bone has been set, a cast helps keep it in place. The cast comes off after the break heals—usually in one to two months.

Banish Bad Bone Habits

You can also keep your bones strong and healthy by avoiding bad habits. Smoking, for example, not only damages your heart and lungs and increases your risk of cancer, it also harms your bones. Smokers may absorb less calcium from foods than nonsmokers. Females who smoke have lower levels of estrogen than those who don't smoke, which can be bad news for the bones.

Alcohol poses another threat to the bones. Heavy drinking can cause bone loss and may lower the body's calcium supply. Excessive drinking can also lead to fractures because heavy drinkers have an increased risk of falling.

Remember, your habits play a big part in the health of your bones. Choosing to eat right and exercise regularly is vital to bone health. Specifically, you need to consume enough calcium and take part in weight-bearing activities. You also need to get enough vitamin D. Avoiding poor nutritional choices and bad habits such as smoking and drinking alcohol excessively also makes a difference. So does wearing the appropriate protective gear during physical activity.

The common element in all of these ways to obtain strong bones is you. What you choose to do and what you choose not to do matters. The actions you take now will affect your bones today, tomorrow, and for a lifetime.

GLOSSARY

amenorrhea The absence of menstruation in a female of reproductive age.

anaphylaxis A sudden, severe, life-threatening allergic reaction that can cause airways to narrow and breathing to become blocked. Other symptoms may include hives, itching, swelling, vomiting, diarrhea, and a drop in blood pressure.

anorexia nervosa A disorder that involves strictly limiting food intake, extreme weight loss, and a distorted self-image.

blood clot A mass of blood that has hardened from a liquid to a solid. A blood clot helps "plug" an injury and stop blood flow.

bone marrow Soft tissue found in the center of the spongy bone that stores fat and produces red and white blood cells and platelets.

bone mass The amount of bone tissue in the skeleton.

bulimia A condition that involves overeating followed by purging. Purging methods include vomiting or the use of laxatives.

calcium A mineral that is needed for strong bones and teeth.

cancellous bone Porous bone tissue that looks like a sponge with many spaces; also known as spongy bone.

cartilage Tough, bendable connective tissue found in joints and at the ends of bones that prevents bones from rubbing together.

collagen A fibrous protein that is found in skin, bone, and connective tissue.

diuretic A drug that increases the discharge of urine.

estrogen A hormone that promotes the growth and normal functioning of the female reproductive system. Estrogen plays a key role in the development of bone density in women.

growth plate The region in a long bone where growth in length occurs.

immobilize To prevent or restrict normal movement with a splint, cast, or other device.

joint The place where two or more bones come together.

lactose A type of sugar that is present in milk and milk products.

lactose intolerance The absence of an enzyme that is needed to digest milk sugar.

laxative A drug that stimulates emptying of the bowels and eases constipation.

ligament A tough, elastic band of tissue that joins bones together at the joints.

osteoporosis A disease that causes bone density to be lost and bones to become so fragile that they break easily.

peak bone mass The amount of bone mass a person has when the skeleton fully matures and the bones have reached their maximum density and strength.

periosteum A thin layer of membrane that is found on the outer surface of all bones except at the joints. This layer is home to blood vessels and cells that work to repair broken bones.

platelet Blood cell that helps create blood clots.

red blood cell Blood cell that helps bring oxygen to all parts of the body.

remodeling A lifelong process in which old bone is removed and new bone is deposited.

sprain A partial tearing of a ligament.

strain The partial tearing of a muscle or tendon.

tendon A cord of tough tissue that connects muscles to bones.

white blood cell Blood cell that fights diseases and infections.

FOR MORE INFORMATION

American Academy of Pediatrics (AAP)
141 Northwest Point Boulevard
Elk Grove Village, IL 60007-1098
(847) 434-4000
Web site: http://www.aap.org
This organization focuses on the health, safety, and well-being of children through education, research, and advocacy. The AAP site offers information on bone health, nutrition, eating disorders, obesity, and a range of health topics associated with childhood and adolescence.

Canadian Orthopaedic Foundation
P.O. Box 7029
Innisfil, ON L9S 1A8
Canada
(416) 410-2341
Web site: http://www.canorth.org
A registered charity, the Canadian Orthopaedic Foundation offers information on how people can build, maintain, and restore their bone and joint health.

National Institute of Arthritis and Musculoskeletal and Skin Diseases (NIAMS)
1 AMS Circle
Bethesda, MD 20892-3675
(877) 226-4267
Web site: http://www.niams.nih.gov

Along with informing the public about research on diseases that involve bones and muscles, NIAMS offers information on maintaining bone health.

National Osteoporosis Foundation (NOF)
1150 17th Street NW
Suite 850
Washington, DC 20036
(800) 231-4222
Web site: http://www.nof.org/home
NOF offers information on the prevention of osteoporosis and broken bones and promotes strong bones for life. The organization works to reduce human suffering through programs of public awareness, education, advocacy, and research.

NIH Osteoporosis and Related Bone Diseases—National Resource Center
2 AMS Circle
Bethesda, MD 20892-3676
(800) 624-BONE [2663]
Web site: http://www.bones.nih.gov
A part of the U.S. Department of Health and Human Services, the center provides information and resources about osteoporosis and other metabolic bone diseases. The center works to enhance knowledge and understanding of the prevention, early detection, and treatment of these diseases as well as strategies for coping with them.

Osteoporosis Canada
1090 Don Mills Road, Suite 301
Toronto, ON M3C 3R6
Canada
(416) 696-2663
Web site: http://www.osteoporosis.ca
Osteoporosis Canada, a registered charity, serves people who have, or
are at risk for, osteoporosis. The organization aims to educate people about this disease, including how to reduce the risk of getting it.

President's Council on Fitness, Sports & Nutrition (PCFSN)
1101 Wootton Parkway, Suite 560
Rockville, MD 20852
(240) 276-9567
Web sites: http://www.fitness.gov; http://www.presidentschallenge.org
PCFSN aims to promote healthy lifestyles for all Americans by provid-
ing information regarding the benefits of good nutrition, physical
activity, and sports participation. The council cosponsors the
President's Challenge, an exercise program open to people of all
ages and abilities.

Web Sites

Due to the changing nature of Internet links, Rosen Publishing has
developed an online list of Web sites related to the subject of this book.
This site is updated regularly. Please use this link to access the list:

http://www.rosenlinks.com/hab/skel

Abramovitz, Melissa. *Osteoporosis* (Diseases and Disorders). Detroit, MI: Lucent Books, 2011.

Ballard, Carol. *Bones: Injury, Illness, and Health* (Body Focus). Chicago, IL: Heinemann Library, 2009.

Ballard, Carol. *What Happens to Broken Bones?* (Inside My Body). Chicago, IL: Raintree, 2011.

Burstein, John. *The Mighty Muscular and Skeletal Systems: How Do My Bones and Muscles Work?* St. Catharines, ON, Canada: Crabtree, 2009.

Cobb, Vicki, Dennis Kunkel, and Andrew Harris. *Your Body Battles a Broken Bone.* Minneapolis, MN: Millbrook Press, 2009.

Cohen, Marina. *Why We Need Vitamins* (Science of Nutrition). New York, NY: Crabtree, 2011.

Faigenbaum, Avery D., and Wayne L. Westcott. *Youth Strength Training: Programs for Health, Fitness, and Sport*. Champaign, IL: Human Kinetics, 2009.

Haywood, Karen. *Skeletal System* (The Amazing Human Body). New York, NY: Marshall Cavendish Children, 2009.

Hoffman, Gretchen. *Osteoporosis* (Health Alert). New York, NY: Marshall Cavendish Benchmark, 2008.

Jenkins, Steve. *Bones: Skeletons and How They Work.* New York, NY: Scholastic Press, 2010.

Markle, Sandra. *Shattered Bones: True Survival Stories* (Powerful Medicine). Minneapolis, MN: Lerner Publications, 2011.

McCarthy, Rose. *Food Labels: Using Nutrition Information to Create a Healthy Diet* (Library of Nutrition). Rev. ed. New York, NY: Rosen Central, 2008.

Olhoff, Jim. *Muscles and Bones* (You're the Doctor). Edina, MN: ABDO Publishing, 2012.

Petrie, Kristin. *The Skeletal System* (Checkerboard Science Library). Edina, MN: ABDO Publishing, 2007.

Rake, Jody Sullivan. *The Human Skeleton* (Fact Finders). Mankato, MN: Capstone Press, 2010.

Roza, Greg. *The Skeletal System* (The Human Body). New York, NY: Gareth Stevens Publishing, 2012.

Sertori, Trisha. *Dairy Foods* (Body Fuel for Healthy Bodies). New York, NY: Marshall Cavendish Benchmark, 2008.

Snedden, Robert. *Understanding Muscles and the Skeleton* (Understanding the Human Body). New York, NY: Rosen Central, 2010.

Watson, Stephanie. *Vitamins and Minerals: Getting the Nutrients Your Body Needs.* New York, NY: Rosen Publishing, 2011.

American Academy of Orthopaedic Surgeons. "Female Athletes: Health Problems Caused by Extreme Exercise and Dieting." October 2009. Retrieved June 8, 2011 (http://orthoinfo.aaos.org/topic.cfm?topic=A00342).

American Academy of Orthopaedic Surgeons. "A Guide to Safety for Young Athletes." October 2007. Retrieved June 9, 2011 (http://orthoinfo.aaos.org/topic.cfm?topic=A00307).

American Academy of Orthopaedic Surgeons. "Recreational Activities and Childhood Injuries." October 2007. Retrieved June 10, 2011 (http://orthoinfo.aaos.org/topic.cfm?topic=A00042).

American Academy of Pediatrics. "Strength Training." HealthyChildren.org, 2011. Retrieved June 7, 2011(http://www.healthychildren.org/English/healthy-living/sports/pages/Strength-Training.aspx?nfstatus=401&nftoken=00000000-0000-0000-0000-000000000000&nfstatusdescription=ERROR%3a+No+local+token).

Fahmy, Sam. "Study Suggests Link Between Obesity, Poor Bone Health." University of Georgia Office of Public Affairs, November 26, 2007. Retrieved June 9, 2011(http://news.uga.edu/releases/article/study-suggests-link-between-obesity-poor-bone-health/).

Faigenbaum, Avery D. "Youth Strength Training: Top 5 Myths." StrongKid.com, 2010. Retrieved June 10, 2011(http://www.strongkid.com/Education___Resources.html).

Mayo Foundation for Medical Education and Research. "Lactose Intolerance." MayoClinic.com, February 16, 2010. Retrieved August 12, 2011 (http://www.mayoclinic.com/health/lactose-intolerance/DS00530).

Mayo Foundation for Medical Education and Research. "Milk Allergy." MayoClinic.com, August 11, 2011. Retrieved August 12, 2011 (http://www.mayoclinic.com/health/milk-allergy/DS01008).

Mayo Foundation for Medical Education and Research. "Osteoporosis." MayoClinic.com, November 20, 2010. Retrieved June 10, 2011 (http://www.mayoclinic.com/health/osteoporosis/DS00128).

Mayo Foundation for Medical Education and Research. "Strength Training: OK for Kids?" MayoClinic.com, January 9, 2010. Retrieved June 7, 2011 (http://www.mayoclinic.com/health/strength-training/HQ01010).

Mayo Foundation for Medical Education and Research."Tips to Bone Up on Bone Health." MayoClinic.com, February 9, 2011. Retrieved August 8, 2011 (http://www.mayoclinic.org/news2011-mchi/6168.html).

National Institute of Arthritis and Musculoskeletal and Skin Diseases. "Growth Plate Injuries." August 2007. Retrieved June 10, 2011 (http://www.niams.nih.gov/Health_Info/Growth_Plate_Injuries/default.asp).

National Institute of Arthritis and Musculoskeletal and Skin Diseases. "Healthy Bones Matter." January 2011. Retrieved June 6, 2011 (http://www.niams.nih.gov/Health_Info/Kids/healthy_bones.asp).

National Institute of Child Health and Human Development. "Milk Matters Calcium Education Campaign—For Health Care Providers: Building Strong Bones." Retrieved June 8, 2011 (http://www.nichd.nih.gov/milk/providers/bones.cfm).

National Institute of Child Health and Human Development. "Milk Matters Calcium Education Campaign—Why Are the Tween and Teen Years So Critical?" Retrieved June 8, 2011 (http://www.nichd.nih.gov/milk/prob/critical.cfm).

National Osteoporosis Foundation. "How the Foods You Eat Affect Your Bones." 2011. Retrieved June 6, 2011 (http://www.nof.org/node/52).

The Nemours Foundation. "The Facts About Broken Bones." KidsHealth.org, August 2009. Retrieved June 10, 2011 (http://kidshealth.org/kid/ill_injure/aches/broken_bones.html).

The Nemours Foundation. "Your Bones." KidsHealth.org, August 2009. Retrieved June 7, 2011(http://kidshealth.org/kid/htbw/bones.html#).

NIH Osteoporosis and Related Bone Diseases—National Resource Center. "Kids and Their Bones: A Guide for Parents." January 2011. Retrieved June 8, 2011 (http://www.niams.nih.gov/Health_Info/Bone/Bone_Health/Juvenile/default.asp).

Office of Dietary Supplements, National Institutes of Health. "Dietary Supplement Fact Sheet: Vitamin D." Retrieved October 11, 2011 (http://ods.od.nih.gov/factsheets/VitaminD-QuickFacts).

Rogers, Paul. "Children Benefit from Weight Training Too." About.com, March 31, 2007. Retrieved June 7, 2011 (http://weighttraining.about.com/od/weighttrainingforgroups/qt/kids_weights.htm).

Ross, A. Catharine. "DRIs for Calcium and Vitamin D." Institute of Medicine of the National Academies, November 30, 2010. Retrieved October 12, 2011 (http://www.iom.edu/Reports/2010/Dietary-Reference-Intakes-for-Calcium-and-Vitamin-D/DRI-Values.aspx).

Simon, Seymour. *Bones: Our Skeletal System*. New York, NY: HarperTrophy, 2000.

U.S. Department of Health and Human Services. *The 2004 Surgeon General's Report on Bone Health and Osteoporosis: What It Means to You*. U.S. Department of Health and Human Services, Office of the Surgeon General, 2004.

U.S. Food and Drug Administration. "Consumer Information—The Food Label and You—New Video." September 8, 2011. Retrieved October 12, 2011 (http://www.fda.gov/Food/LabelingNutrition/ConsumerInformation/ucm246815.htm).

INDEX

About the Author

Maria DaSilva-Gordon keeps her bones strong and healthy by lifting weights, running, and eating calcium-rich foods. Always one to wear appropriate protective gear when being physically active, she has never broken a bone. She writes for various publications, including newspapers and trade journals. She also teaches journalism work-shops to students of various learning abilities and grade levels through her business, Making Headlines, LLC.

Photo Credits

Cover (girl) Lifesize/Thinkstock; cover, back cover, interior background (curly design frame) © istockphoto.com/liquidplanet; cover, interior background (ekg) © istockphoto.com/linearcurves; pp. 4–5 Anatoliy Samara/Shutterstock.com; p. 9 Alila Sao Mai/Shutterstock.com; p. 11 http://www.niams.nih.gov/Health_Info/Kids/healthy_bones.asp; p. 13 Alan Boyde/Visuals Unlimited/Getty Images; p. 17 Image Source/Getty Images; p. 18 Tom Grill/Photographer's Choice/Getty Images; p. 19 Fuse/Getty Images; p. 22 Design Pics/Stock Foundry/Valueline/Thinkstock; p. 24 © Richard B. Levine/Newscom; p. 26 Image Source/Getty Images; p. 30 Preston Keres/The Washington Post/Getty Images; p. 32 Chris Clinton/Digital Vision/Thinkstock; pp. 34, 39 Hemera/Thinkstock; p. 40 Doug Menuez/Photodisc/Thinkstock; p. 44 iStockphoto/Thinkstock; pp. 46–47 John Moore/Getty Images; p. 48 Ebby May/Taxi/Getty Images.

Designer: Nicole Russo; Editor: Andrea Sclarow Paskoff;
Photo Researcher: Amy Feinberg

Discarded

Per RFP 03764 Follett School Solutions guarantees
hardcover bindings through SY 2024-2025
877.899.8550 or customerservice@follett.com